STENCIL
SOURCE BOOK

STENCIL
SOURCE BOOK

OVER 200 STENCILS TO MAKE
FOR ALL AROUND THE HOME

PATRICIA MEEHAN

NORTH
LIGHT
BOOKS

CINCINNATI, OHIO

First published in Great Britain in 1993 by
Anaya Publishers Ltd, London

First published in the United States by North Light Books,
F&W Publications, Inc., 1507 Dana Avenue, Cincinnati, Ohio 45207
1-800-289-0963

Editor: Janet Donin
Designer: Sheila Volpe
Special Photography: Les Meehan
Artwork: Michael Volpe,
Tony Bellue
Coral Mula

ISBN 0-89134-586-8

Typeset by Servis Filmsetting Ltd, Manchester
Colour reproduction by J. Film Process, Singapore
Printed and bound in Malaysia by Times Offset Ltd

CONTENTS

INTRODUCTION

In the following pages I want to show you just how versatile stencilling can be. You can stencil virtually anything from floors and walls to ceramics and silk. No matter what your lifestyle, no matter what your surroundings, you can make stencilling work for you. Stencilling is not difficult to master. With imagination, a few tools and very little outlay you can give your home unique touches to set it apart from the rest. You will also have the added satisfaction of knowing that these touches are yours and yours alone. One of the beauties of stencilling is that two people, using the same design and the same paints, will invariably produce different results.

Each chapter in this book is devoted to a different decorative theme. Within each chapter you will find many creative ideas to adapt for your own use. Some of them are simple, some quite ambitious. At the end of each chapter you will find a selection of designs to trace off and use. Although the designs are grouped into specific themes, try to view them in a more general way. For instance, the pineapple in the Rustic Charm chapter would be just as much at home in the Kitchen Garden section. It is up to you to use them as you wish.

Many of the photographs illustrate items decorated with designs taken from the book. I hope they will give you a taste of what is possible and inspire you to try them for yourself.

Stencils are the most adaptable of decorative tools. Even the simplest border or motif can form the basis for many more designs, all of which will co-ordinate with the original design.

There is one golden rule to follow when you begin to stencil and that is to use restraint. The temptation is always there to add just one more motif, but you should know when to stop. This is not always easy when you are heady with your new-found success. However, your stencilling should blend into its surroundings to become a part of the room rather than shout at you from the walls. The ideas in this book are there for you to dip into at will. Use them to create a completely new look to your home or merely to give strength to an existing decorative theme.

A recent visitor to my home asked if she could see some of my stencilling. I took this to be a great compliment as she had just walked past some of my rather large projects.

The last part of the book deals with the instructions. Here you will learn about the materials, how to apply the colours and how to design and cut your own stencils. If you are new to stencilling it's a good idea to read this section before you attempt any projects of your own. Even if you have stencilled before, there may be something new for you there. But remember, when looking for source material for designs, the copyright laws protect other people's work.

Now all you have to do, is join in the fun and pick up a brush, choose your colours and start stencilling.

An airy conservatory takes on a dramatic and colourful look with this jazzy stencil treatment.

Chapter 1

TRULY ROMANTIC

*Do you love poetry and romantic novels?
Do you love frills and flounces; antique lace
and ribbons; dried flowers from a favourite
bouquet and photographs or curls of hair in
lockets? If the answer is yes then you are a
true romantic.*

PREVIOUS PAGE Here is a bedroom with all the trappings of romance: old beams, draped fabric, fresh flowers and golden cherubs looking down onto the pillows. Add your own stencil decoration and you have a room to dream in.

In days gone by, every lady of quality had her own boudoir which quite literally means a 'sulking room'. It was a room decorated as she wished, where she could keep all her favourite belongings. Here she could sit and read poetry, embroider or paint watercolours while dreaming her dreams.

To have a room of your own is something few of us can afford these days. However with a little bit of stencilling you can add those special touches to your home that will bring a little romance back into your life.

There is no better place to start than the bedroom. Here you can let your romantic nature take full flight. Stencil a floral swag around the walls at ceiling height and add a smaller, co-ordinating border, at dado rail level. Put matching motifs onto glass lampshades and watch the soft light shine through.

You can buy lots of inexpensive butter muslin and add a stencil motif to give your bedroom a soft, dreamy quality. You can drape it quite simply above your bed over curtain poles suspended from the ceiling, or make complex swags and bows.

There are many ways to make your windows extra special too. You can buy plain fabric and add your own pattern to match the decoration in the rest of the room. This fabric can also be used to make ordinary curtains or fancy blinds. Stencil butter muslin with ribbons, flowers and butterflies. Use a creamy white fabric paint on muslin and you have, what I like to think of as instant antique lace! This can look quite stunning hanging at the window from shiny brass poles and is a feature that you can carry into all the rooms in your home.

Here fabric paint has been used to stencil a rose motif onto swathes of butter muslin. The light, airiness of the fabric makes the design appear to float on the breeze.

What could be more simple than a pot-pourri bag? A touch of stencilling, some ribbon and lace and you have unashamed romance. This would make an ideal gift for a special friend. Using the same idea you could make pillows filled with herbs to help you drift gently off to sleep.

This bed has been decorated at the head and inner base with a heart-shaped wreath designed with pastel coloured flowers intertwined with ribbon. The pillowcases have been decorated to match.

Why not turn your attention to the bedroom furniture? Stencil a floral motif onto the top of your dressing table with smaller versions of the design on the drawer fronts. You can even stencil the drawer knobs with tiny flowers or hearts. Your wardrobe may benefit from a design within the panels and your bed can be transformed if you stencil onto the bed head and base. If you have a modern bed with no head-board you can make your own. Just stencil onto large cushion pads and hang them with ribbons from a brass or wooden pole fixed to the wall behind the bed. Even the shades on your bedside lights can be stencilled.

Chests of drawers, whether old or new, are an ideal surface on which to stencil. This new pine chest was first colourwashed, then stencilled on each drawer front. The trailing. flooral design echos the curtains and cleverly alternates with each drawer.

If you stencil onto fabrics you can make your own matching bed linen. What could be prettier than a motif on your pillowcases and small sprigs of flowers on the sheets or duvet cover? If you really want to splash out you could make a bedcover in raw silk and stencil it with a pattern radiating out from the centre.

There are many small touches you can make to your room that will add to the romantic mood. Stencil onto picture mounts and frames, lampshades and even your night-clothes. These are all affordable and are indeed the finishing touches.

The bathroom is another area in which to indulge your romantic nature. Bathrooms can often look, if not feel, quite cold so try softening the appearance of your walls with a paint technique, before you start to stencil. Rag rolling and sponging produce wonderful surfaces for stencilling as they add depth to the designs.

Put a plain oval mirror on the wall and stencil a pretty floral design around it, perhaps with some of the flowers spilling onto the glass. Decorate your walls with pictures hung from stencilled bows and ribbons. The same ribbon design could also be used as a border around the walls at picture rail height.

If you have a wood panelled bath you have another area for stencilling. Or, if you're lucky enough to own an old fashioned, roll-top bath you can stencil onto the undersides. And why not add the soft touch of a quilted bath mat? You can make this quite simply with stencilled fabric, padding and a non-slip backing material.

Inspiration for romantic designs are all around you. Look at birthday cards, wrapping paper, collections of old valentines and the paper 'cuts' used for decoupage. Maybe you have a favourite brooch or piece of lace from which you

can take your own special design.

Sit down and write a list of the things that you find romantic. At the same time write a list of the colours that you associate with a romantic mood. This will give you a personal colour scheme. You may prefer soft, dreamy pastels in pale blue, pink, cream, apricot or lilac. On the other hand you may decide to use more vibrant colours such as emerald green, bright blue or shocking pink.

Never forget, this is your stencilling so you make the decisions. The choice is all yours.

An old picture postcard or family photo looks so pretty in an oval frame especially with stencilled flowers decorating the mount. You could also design a floral picture and decorate the mount with a smaller version of the design.

The lily of the valley motif shown here would make a beautiful frieze around a bedroom wall. To ring the changes you could reverse the stencil at alternate applications. Sweet peas are a favourite flower with everyone and would look delightful stencilled onto bed linen. Use this posy scattered over a plain duvet cover but use only the flower heads to decorate the pillowcases.

The honeysuckle motif can be split into two distinct elements. Stencil the flower heads in bunches around the wall and the ribbon around the bed head. The whole design would also look attractive as a surround for a pretty picture. The heart and ribbon and pansy motifs would look pretty decorating small keepsake boxes.

My pretty heart and flower design is ideal for a bedroom door perhaps with the occupant's name stencilled within the heart. Or why not use this design to decorate a wedding or anniversary card with the couple's names in the centre. A double bow stencilled on the wall just above a picture, or over a mirror will give it a special look. And this exotic lily could form a magnificent border around a bath with the motif used back-to-back over the washbasin and mirror. A simple ribbon border stencilled at picture rail height, or surrounding a collection of favourite photographs would give a special look to your room. And don't forget to pattern your sheets and pillowcases for a truly romantic feel.

Roses and leaves are the perfect motif to stencil onto drawer fronts. Stencilled, in a creamy colour, onto butter muslin this design becomes a wonderful imitation of lace. The simple flower border would look pretty stencilled at dado rail height with the blooms scattered randomly below. Use the spray of flowers to decorate plain curtains with matching tie backs. The daisy motif would be ideal around a bedroom door. Hearts and flowers are always the symbol of romance so what better design to use on wrapping paper and cards for your loved ones?

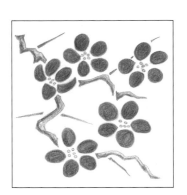

Chapter 2

EXOTIC EAST

*Sumptuous silks, cords and tassels;
kimonos and mist-shrouded mountains;
mythical beasts and flamboyant flowers.
These are just a few of the images conjured
up by the exotic East. On the other hand,
a simple decorative style may be brought to
mind where both furniture and decoration
are kept to a minimum. The East has
always been an enigma, a land cloaked in
wondrous mystery.*

When early explorers first opened the trade routes to the Far East they introduced a wealth of new and exciting imagery to the western world. Imagine seeing exquisitely patterned kimonos and silks, beautifully lacquered boxes, oriental pots and vases and new vibrant species of flowers, all for the first time.

The Japanese were masters of the art of stencilling, their ties or bridges often being made from a single strand of silk. Some examples of these early stencils and the stencilled goods they produced still remain and are much sought after today.

There are two contrasting styles of oriental design. One highly decorative and the other very simple with just one or two beautiful items in a room. This second style would fit easily into many modern homes with their clean lines and sleek furniture.

A bathroom would be just the place to indulge yourself with eastern imagery. Stencil a border of waterlilies around the bath then add sparkling dragonflies in metallic paints alighting on the blooms. And just imagine the carp design swimming through watery swirls. You could even use all three to stunning effect with the golden carp under water, the waterlilies floating on the surface and the dragonflies in the air.

If you feel nervous about introducing this style to your home, start by making a set of sumptuous cushions patterned with exotic blooms. Simple flower designs look marvellous on plain sofas and chairs or within a bustling floral scheme.

The fan is a favourite motif from the East and can be adapted in many ways to decorate your home. Make a stencil of the fan. It need not be complicated,

This wooden box was painted with several coats of maroon paint before the oriental motifs and dragonfly were added using gold, metallic acrylic paint. The box would look equally good with a black or bright blue base colour.

These cushions were stencilled with floral motifs in a cheerful selection of colours to bring interest to a cane peacock chair and are an easy way to bring a touch of the orient into your home. If you prefer, use silk or unbleached calico for the covers.

The carp on the sides of this lantern appear to be swimming through the air and take on a luminous quality when the light is on. You can make this lamp yourself but do take care and use the correct materials.

only a few lines are required to give the proper effect. Colour in these lines and then make a motif to fill the interior space. This shape would also give you an ideal opportunity to use the reverse stencilling technique. The fans can then be used in various sizes as borders or motifs on furniture, walls and fabric.

Fitted cushions for wicker chairs in your garden or conservatory would be an ideal place to show off your skills. You could surround your furniture with plants and exotic blooms to enhance the mood.

Using more simple imagery, stencil either a roller blind or a roman blind and let the light shine through.

Take a wooden tray, paint it black and stencil it with your chosen design in gold paint. Then add coats of varnish, until you have a gleaming imitation of lacquer ware. After this success you may wish to tackle a larger piece of furniture such as a table, chest of drawers or a trunk.

OPPOSITE *What could be more exotic and magical than the dragon? Stencilled here in stark black on white, it is offset beautifully by the wavy design just above the skirting.*

BELOW *Here two stencils were used, one for the columns and another for the arches. The tile like quality of the design contrasts dramatically with the exotic floral stencil patterning the day bed.*

Stencilling silk is a delightful way to produce exotic wall hangings for your home. You could make a set of floral hangings for your sitting room or create small scenes such as the one on the coffee table at the start of this chapter. Of course you could always stencil them directly onto the walls. Or why not stencil a silken kimono or dressing gown with your favourite eastern motif?

If you live in a home with minimalist furnishings you could try a very different approach. A magnificently stencilled ikebana flower arrangement or a bonsai tree or even a delicate figurine could become the focal point of a room, especially if lit with a single spotlight.

There are countless sources of inspiration for your own designs. Visit your local library to find books on oriental art, pottery or gardening. Browse through a book on ikebana and you could find yourself stencilling a flower arrangement that needs no attention and will never die. Travel books will also provide a wealth of architectural detail from which you can produce more simplistic geometric patterns.

As the decorative ideals of the orient are based on the natural world and flowing design, you cannot fail to find a design to suit your home.

The heron is a typical oriental decoration and I think it would make a spectacular wall hanging with a floral or geometric border. Alternatively he could be designed to 'walk' along your bath panel.

The dragonflies will make an unusual border on their own but could also be introduced to any of the floral designs to give movement and interest. Use metallic colours for these insects to make them zing. You could use the bamboo design on a set of curtains with a small matching border in shades of green for a calm and peaceful effect.

Carp could swim lazily around your bathroom walls but why not do the unexpected and stencil them onto a glass-topped coffee table with car spray paints? Don't forget to cut an extra registered overlay for the eye.

The double border of flowers and leaves could also be used as a single line for smaller projects.

Give your sheets and pillowcases a new and exotic look with the chrysanthemum using oranges and reds typical of the orient. It could also be used to make simple pictures. Stencil the motif onto a piece of rice paper using bright colours, then add one of the symbols in black. Stencil waterlilies in the bathroom coloured black and gold or use more natural colours on a set of cushions. The hibiscus motif is pretty enough to adorn a silk kimono while the more masculine symbols could be used on a dressing gown.

28

Chapter 3

RUSTIC CHARM

Wood-burning fires; bellows and toasting forks; rocking chairs and footstools; flowers both fresh and dried; brightly patterned rugs on polished wooden floors and patchwork quilts. To all this add the sound of a clock ticking quietly on the wall and you cannot fail to imagine the rural idyll of peace and tranquillity.

This charming wall decoration was made quite easily by stencilling a floral circlet onto a piece of lightweight plywood. The outer and inner edges were then cut away using a fretsaw. This idea could be extended to many different motifs and, by leaving in the centres, you would have a very original set of place mats.

Everyone has their own imagined, rural haven whether it be an English cottage and garden, mountain chalet, stone villa, or the rustic log cabin of North America.

Unfortunately, not all of us will be able to turn the dream into reality as far as the location is concerned, but there are many small details you can introduce into your home with stencilling, to enhance your surroundings and add to the illusion of country life with all its charms.

Stencilling was very popular in the early pioneering days of America. Itinerant stencillers toured the towns and villages plying their trade. They used home-made paints to decorate the walls of the settlers' homes with the popular motifs of the day. The tools of these artisans proved to be very durable and some of the original brushes and stencils are still in existence today.

Love birds on branches, stylised trees and the pineapple, the traditional symbol of hospitality, were all sten-cilled onto walls and tin-ware. In those days, ornaments were a rarity and everything in the house had to be useful. So an inexpensive, homespun, form of decoration was used by all, while fancy goods were only supplied by the wagon trains.

Colourwashed walls, prettily stencilled with small flowers have a delightful country cottage look. And if you're feeling ambitious why not stencil some decorative china to match?

The key to rustic charm, therefore, is simplicity. And what better place to begin than by stencilling the fabrics in your home? Decorate panels of net with flowers and butterflies; stencil stylised flowers onto cushions or new loose covers for your sofa and chairs; make a patchwork quilt by stencilling a suit-able combination of motifs onto a large piece of fabric then hand or machine quilt the end result. If all this is too ambitious, start with a set of cushions using the same method. You can; of course; stencil individual pieces of material and make your own really original quilt in the traditional manner.

Lovebirds, hearts and stylised trees are typical of rustic charm and are the perfect decorative feature for this simple blanket box.

Now think of what you can do to your furniture. Rocking chairs cry out for stencilling on their seats and backs as do dining chairs. Stencil the chair itself or make seat covers in a plain fabric so that you can add the finishing touches with your brush. It can be interesting to buy striped material and stencil small motifs either onto or in-between the stripes.

If you have a fireplace why not stencil around it with a simple design? You don't have to use the motif in a straight line but make it billow in places. When you reach the chimney breast you can make a circlet with your chosen design and stencil initials and dates inside for instant antiquity.

Hang dried flowers on walls and in between stencil with bunches of herbs.

The rocking chair is quite old and well used as you can see by its shiny seat, as such it is the perfect foil for the simple flower and leaf decoration.

Turn your attention to the outside of the house and make a pretty name or number plate for your home. Display either on the gate, porch or door and stencil a matching motif on your mailbox.

Think about the colours you will use. Look at the photograph at the beginning of this chapter, you will see that the fireplace is decorated with acorns and oak leaves in autumnal colours. Imagine the difference if a design of spring flowers had been used, painted in blues, pinks and leafy greens.

Take a walk down a country lane in spring and you will find a wealth of inspiration for stencil designs such as primroses, bluebells, wild daffodils and the colours of new buds. Take the same walk in summer, autumn and winter and you will find a host of different things to fire your imagination. Foxgloves, cornfields and poppies, fallen leaves and the bare-branched trees of winter can all be adapted for stencil designs.

If it is difficult for you to visit the country, look at books and magazines about the countryside and its wildlife. Seek out books on old-fashioned rural crafts and customs or illustrated books on wild flowers and grasses.

With a little stencilling you will bring your rural dream another step closer to reality and give your home a welcoming atmosphere.

This trug has been coloured blue with a wood stain and decorated with ivy and flower stencils. Now it is not only useful for collecting flowers from the garden but it is also a decorative container for dried flowers.

The flower and leaf ring will brighten up plain tiles in your kitchen or bathroom, but don't forget to varnish them for added protection.

Oak leaves and acorns are a wonderful decorative theme for your winter curtains or a rug. And I like to see them on plain pine furniture as well. The maple leaf and the 'helicopters' can be used to brighten up a very plain wall in a room that needs little decoration, or you could use them for a fun decoration in a child's room. Don't forget to stencil the lines at the sides of each motif as they will add a sense of movement.

The patchwork squares are ideal for non-sewers who hanker after something really traditional. Use them to pattern quilts, cushions or even wooden storage boxes in your kitchen.

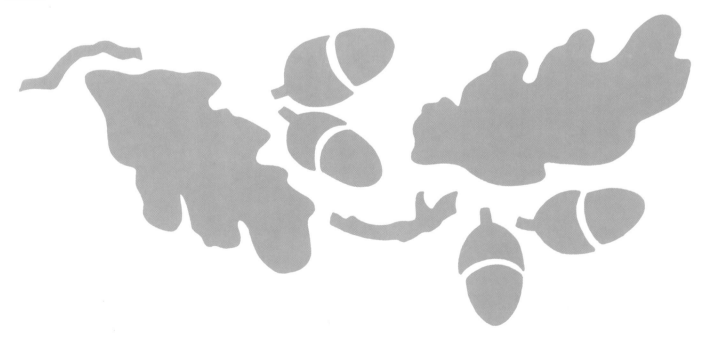

A dainty border of buds will look pretty around a small window or bordering a cushion. If you have wall vases or uplighters, use the ivy together with any floral design to spill out of the container across plain walls. You could also enlarge the design and use it as a stunning border on the floor. Cut a stencil for the main leaf shape and another registered overlay for an inner colour.

The tiny flower border could be used to decorate small picture frames or the edge of a little table.

Decorate your fireplace with the poppy corn dolly by putting one motif at each side of the chimney breast, then use the flower and corn elements of the motif elsewhere in the room.

A pair of lovebirds would look charming decorating your bedroom curtains, or as a symbol of harmony stencilled above the entrance to your home. This pretty flower circlet would make an unusual decoration for living room walls, while the cheerful basket of flowers always looks pretty on kitchen doors. The cockerel and chicken are also a splendid motif for a kitchen – use as a border running along the top of the tiles. Café curtains could be decorated to match, together with small kitchen utensils and jars.

Chapter 4

BABY TALK

Teddy bears and dolls; building bricks and kites; rattles and rocking horses; animals dressed as people; animals who can speak. Everything is possible to a child and it's into this world that you must enter to successfully decorate your child's room.

The stencil of baby bears being held aloft by brightly coloured balloons is an ideal choice for this cot. The size of the motif is varied to give added interest. Simple balloons stencilled onto the side slats are made to look more interesting by the changes in colour.

When you decorate your child's room remember that you are not decorating it for yourself but for your child. So try to provide a stimulating environment that you can change as the child gets older. Good stencilling can produce a room that is not only a delight to look at but also educational.

If you combine pale walls with brightly coloured stencil designs you will give your child the best of both visual worlds. All the designs in this chapter can be brightly coloured. Flowers can change around the wall from palest pink to deep burgundy and a boy rabbit can be wearing a different coloured jacket each time you see him. Why not let your own imagination run riot with blue, red or even green cats on the wall? As long as the image is stimulating your baby won't mind!

Stencil a bright border around the room at dado rail height so that your baby will be able to see it from the cot. It's also a good idea to put a border or a number of motifs near the floor, perhaps running just above the skirting board. After all, your baby will spend a lot of time seeing the world at that level.

Using the alphabet designs from the Festive section you can stencil your baby's name on the wall over the cot or even on the cot itself. This idea comes in useful when you have more than one child as you can personalise each cot and toybox. Of course there are many things to stencil in a nursery besides the walls and furniture. You can put motifs on doors and lampshades, make your own colourful mobile and even make a decorative rug for the floor.

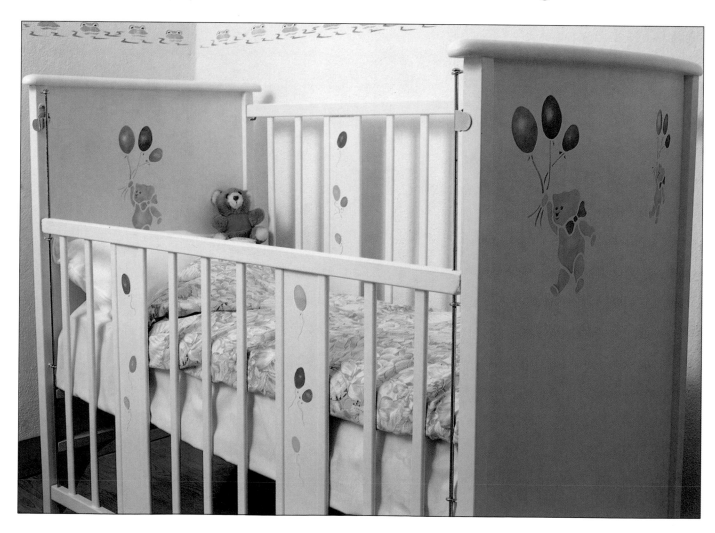

LEFT *The border running around the nursery wall is one I call 'Find the Frog Prince' as only one of the frogs is wearing a crown. It makes an imaginative game for a slightly older child, especially as you can paint over the crown and move it from head to head when you choose.*

BELOW *This simple mobile was made from card, light wooden rods and thread. The clowns' faces and the balloons were stencilled onto both sides of the card – remember to reverse the motif on the back – and then cut out using a sharp craft knife. This is a toy to be looked at and not eaten by your baby so make sure it is out of reach of tiny hands.*

As your child gets older, you can use stencils to play games. A height chart stencilled onto the wall is always fun. And a clock face with moveable cardboard hands pinned to the design will enable you to play a tell-the-time game. You can make a counting game by stencilling a border around the room, at whatever height you choose, of one flower, two cats, and three ducks. Another learning game is to stencil a letter on the wall followed by an object the name of which starts with that initial letter. For example the letter D followed by a stencilled dog. And if you're feeling really ambitious you could make a poster on a large sheet of cardboard using the whole alphabet. I'm sure your children will find these instant counting and recognition games great fun!

Cheeky soft toys peep out of a toybox. The box is decorated with motifs of both boy and girl rabbits. The colourways of their clothing changes at each repeat of the motif. A row of bright yellow ducks walk along the edge between pretty, coloured flowers.

Of course, the room does not have to be wholly educational. If your child has a favourite toy, use that as a basis for decoration. A stencilled doll can be made to walk around the room or a little train could chug up and down hills with little puffs of steam coming from its funnel. It's amusing to stencil the ceiling with stars and the man in the moon. If you use fluorescent paints it's even more fun!

As your child gets older and is introduced to the delights of fairy stories and nursery rhymes, you can get a little more adventurous with your ideas. Goldilocks and the Three Bears, Little Boy Blue and Cinderella, are all possible stencilling themes.

To find sources for stencil designs you need only look as far as your local library or the picture books in your own home. Do not worry too much about your drawing capabilities. A stylised teddy or doll will have just as much significance to a small child as the real thing.

Write down a list of all the things that you associate with a carefree childhood no matter how silly they may seem. You may think of spinning tops, kites, bicycles or toy drums. And read some of your favourite childhood books to spark your imagination. For example, you may be surprised at how often food is mentioned in children's stories. Slabs of fruitcake and jam-

Ribbons and bows are always an excellent choice for a baby girl's nursery and the design will remain pleasing for many years.

covered scones, dripping with cream, were always a tea time treat. Animals are another great favourite, from jungle animals peering out of the undergrowth to kittens chasing butterflies. Circuses, holidays and games are also popular themes. As you can see you will have little trouble in finding ideas.

Naturally what is popular with a child today may well be out of favour tomorrow, but through the medium of stencilling you can easily keep up with the trends without any costly redecoration. One way is to create a nursery full of nostalgia with stencilled hobbyhorses, tin soldiers or skipping ropes. These are images that you and your child will want to keep forever. After all wouldn't it be wonderful for your children to grow into adulthood with fond memories of their nursery, stencilled with love and devotion?

47

I have deliberately designed the bunny rabbits as little characters for your children to befriend, so let them decide on the colours for the clothing. Make a separately registered overlay for the eyes, inner ears, noses and buttons.

The bonnet motif would make a pretty border in a little girl's nursery while the bootees could be coloured either blue or pink. The cat is ideal for a skirting board in a child's room, but you may also like to stencil him in your living room, beside the fire or in the kitchen sitting by the back door. The clowns, with their smiling faces, are perfect for a multicoloured room.

49

To give your baby something to look at when he is crawling around the floor, stencil a border of flowerpots around the wall at skirting board height. One extra large plant could become a growing chart, with additional flowers and stems added as your child gets taller. You can also personalise the little figure by painting its rainwear in the same colours as your own child's raincoat and wellingtons. And the little pull-along duck could be a different colour at each repetition.

Teddy bears holding balloons cannot help floating around the walls and may even fly so high they can say hello to the man in the moon! A second registered stencil is necessary for the teddy bear's face. Sand castles and a bucket and spade will help your child to remember happy holidays, and could be stencilled as a border at floor level or used randomly around the walls.

Kites can soar around the room and fly across the ceiling in a riot of colours. The cute little pigs are perfect for trotting around the sides of a toybox, but they could also stand happily on the skirting board. Ducks are always popular with children whether walking around the edges of a small cotton mat or over a bed head. Crossed candysticks and giant lollipops also make colourful motifs for a cot.

You can stencil clusters of frogs on the wall or use them as a simple border.

Chapter 5

MEDITERRANEAN STYLE

Dolphins swimming in sparkling blue seas; olive groves and lizards; vine leaves and shady terraces; golden sunshine and silver moonlit nights; cool white villas festooned with bougainvillaea. All these things and more are reminiscent of the mood of the beautiful Mediterranean.

A wicker sun lounger looks inviting with its brightly stencilled cushions. The decoration is in two parts: the formality of the tile design and the exuberance of the bougainvillaea flowers placed at random within the border.

Everyone dreams of holidaying in a white painted villa, nestling on a cypress-covered hillside, with a balcony overlooking a sapphire blue sea. The villa would be light and airy with tiled floors, cool in the daytime but warm in the evenings. We can't do much about the climate I'm afraid, but you can use colour and creative stencilling to transport a part of the dream into your own home.

The impact of Mediterranean decoration is achieved by the use of rich colours and textures on plain back-grounds. This is the principle to keep in mind when planning your stencilling projects.

It's difficult to achieve texture with stencilling unless you stencil onto textured surfaces. However, if you put your designs onto soft furnishings and furniture you will add the three-dimensionality to create the proper effect.

So where do you start? Probably with the walls. These can be painted in cool colours, white, pale blue or aquamarine for example. You will then have the perfect setting for your designs.

BELOW Five stencil designs work together to produce something a little different. The screen was first rag rolled in pale blue water-based paint. Then I added the mosaic waves and seashells in pearlised acrylics. The sun and stars were stencilled with metallic paints and the dolphins in fast drying stencil paints.

Take a series of designs perhaps on a nautical theme and stencil a large wall hanging directly onto the wall. Many people hang brightly patterned rugs on their walls so why not stencil your own?

A plain bathroom could be brought to life with a frieze of leaping dolphins or flying fish but a more restrained mosaic design in a deep, rich blue would capture the mood just as well.

The people of the Mediterranean spend a great deal of time outside, so the garden is really an extension of the home. If you have garden chairs or loungers you can transform them with new cushions stencilled with your own designs or, try stencilling a wooden garden table with a pattern radiating out from the centre. You may even possess a large umbrella just waiting to be decorated to match your new cushions.

A dining room or outdoor terrace with stencilled grapevines climbing around the walls would make a spectacular backdrop to a convivial evening spent with friends. Table linen and chairs could all be brought into the scheme, decorated with smaller motifs.

Wooden floorboards in a hallway would be the ideal place to stencil a mosaic design. Think big. Don't just use a simple border or motif but look for inspiration at the mosaic floors found in archaeological digs and large museums.

A bedroom could be made to look very glamorous with purple or deep pink bougainvillaea trailing around the walls. Drape a stencilled mosquito net over your bed and echo the design on billowing white curtains at your windows and you will be immediately transported to sunnier climes.

Don't forget ceilings when thinking about stencilling. Clouds, suns, moons and stars are an obvious choice, especially if you are lucky enough to have high ceilings but in smaller rooms try stencilling a large plant on a wall

A tablecloth stencilled with entwined grapes and vine leaves makes a perfect backdrop for continental breakfast to be taken either indoors or on a sunny terrace.

and carry it up to the ceiling to give the impression of height.

Indoor shutters are very reminiscent of the Mediterranean and are an ideal surface for stencil decoration. Trailing plants, birds and butterflies even lizards could capture the atmosphere beautifully.

Clothing bought especially to wear on holiday, is often much brighter than our normal, everyday wardrobe. So bear this in mind when selecting your colours for stencilling. Splashes of bright sea blue, the rich orangey red of the trumpet vine, the kaleidoscope of colours in a Mediterranean sunset – all these and more will bring your decorative ideas to life.

Holiday brochures are an obvious starting point for other reference material, especially those advertising rental villas. Your own holiday photographs could also provide a very personal point of reference. And you'll find lots of books showing the interior design characteristics of different countries. Here you will find interior and exterior architectural styles, both ancient and modern. Books on subjects as diverse as archaeology, sea life and flora and fauna will also provide a framework from which to start.

Painters and sculptors have long been drawn to the Mediterranean for inspiration so why not look at, and enjoy art books to appreciate various artists' impressions of the Mediterranean and all its many colours?

A collection of plates decorated with stylised motifs brighten up a mantelpiece. The lizards escaping from the plate on the right add a touch of humour to the scene.

Lizards in shades of green, brown and turquoise abound in hot climates and would look intriguing running out from behind a plant pot in your sun room. The grape and vine leaf border stencilled around a doorway would be very pretty. Don't forget that vine leaves go through many changes of colour in their growing season, from bright green to red and yellow.

The bathroom is, of course, the ideal place for brightly coloured fish, dolphins, sailboats and waves. But you could adapt the waves mosaic as wall border or as a bath surround on the floor.

A motif of bougainvillaea flowers could decorate anything from a wall border to your soft furnishings.

Again shells and seahorses do belong in the bathroom but if these designs appeal to you try using them to decorate cushions and duvets. Pearlised acrylic paints will give them a beautiful shimmering effect.

The classical urn is a rather unusual motif for a stencil but could be the basis of some very dramatic designs. Colour the bowl in varying shades of terracotta.

The sun motif could also be used virtually anywhere to dispel those gloomy winter moods.

Chapter 6

SIMPLE DESIGN

Chequered tiles and Shaker style; chairs by Rennie Mackintosh and cut glass vases; gingham curtains and white porcelain cups; snowflake crystals and Art Deco. Stencilling does not have to be just flowery, frilly designs. If you prefer clean, uncluttered lines there are many stencil patterns to suit your taste.

PREVIOUS PAGE A simple border stencil has been used in a variety of ways to turn a piece of furniture into a smart games cupboard. The colours I have used are typical of the style, but jade and black, blue and gold or lilac and grey would instantly give the cupboard a new identity.

After the First World War much of the art, architecture and decorative goods produced were more simplistic in style than those of the Victorian era. New schools of thought were heavily biased towards the functional – decoration was a pointless exercise! If an article had simple lines and performed its task, it was considered both beautiful and a work of art! Geometric designs, glass and chrome all became commonplace and as mass production became even more a part of our economy, so decorative pieces disappeared.

Once you start researching this style you will find many ways to stencil your home with simple, clear designs that will act as a background to your furnishings. Even the minimalist may find that one inspired stencil motif could be the focal point in a simple furnishing scheme.

Doorways take on a new character with the addition of an Art Deco border. A design like this could be carried along the wall at skirting board or dado rail level, with single motifs used around the room.

Checks are synonymous with this simple style. Design a border stencil using a single row or many rows of checks depending on the size of your room. When you are satisfied with the design you will have to decide whether to position the border at dado rail height, half way up the wall, or at picture rail height towards the ceiling.

You could of course stencil the design, as a border, on a wooden floor having adjusted its size accordingly. This chequered design would fit equally well into any room in the house, but I think it would work particularly well in the bathroom, kitchen or play room, changing the size and colour as you think necessary.

Taking the idea of a checked floor one step further, you could add chess pieces for a unique and dramatic, black and white design.

67

Simple designs can also add sophistication to a room, especially the Art Deco designs consisting of three different elements like my rialto, semicircles and corner designs. Stencil any one of these designs as a border around the room at whatever height you choose. Colour the first and largest element black, the second grey and the third, smallest element, shocking pink or jade to give instant impact! With a grey carpet, black or white furniture and the addition of toning silk cushions on the chairs, the impact would still be there, but the stencilling would recede into the background to merely complement the scheme.

A streamlined, modern kitchen could be decorated with the same sleek motifs. A rose garland would look totally out of place, but a stylised flower design with triangular petals, and therefore geometric in appearance, would look more at home.

ABOVE Plain roller blinds are a practical buy, but if you feel in need of a change you can cheer them up with crisp, candy colours like these. Use other colours such as black, gold and grey to give an altogether different appearance.

RIGHT Even small items like this letter rack can look striking when decorated with a simple motif and you could use the same motif to personalise your stationery. These make ideal projects for beginners as they are quick and easy to produce.

There are many geometrically patterned rugs available but you may find it more satisfying to stencil your own directly onto floorboards. An ideal location would be in the dining room giving you a spill and stain proof area directly beneath the table, a definite bonus if you have young children or clumsy guests. Copy the same design on a lampshade suspended over the table to tie the scheme together. Simple designs could extend to the curtain edges or even blinds.

On the other hand classical designs like the Greek key may have a more masculine appeal. White walls with turquoise linen and a design in navy blue would look very stylish. Or what about creamy walls and bedding with a black and gold design on the walls and sheets? The possibilities are endless.

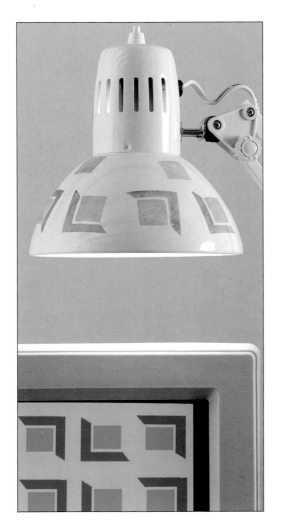

You can find ideas for design all around you. Everyday sights like brick walls and roofing tiles would easily convert to simple patterns. Books on exterior architecture and post-war furniture would provide useful references, and books on Art Deco and the Bauhaus movement abound. Perhaps you have a piece of jewellery or an ornament from which to take a motif. If you have small children, why not look at their artistic endeavours with new eyes? Inspiration is all around just waiting to be seen.

A simple stencil in a single colour, positioned at random on a brilliantly coloured wall surface, gives a crisp yet eye-catching effect.

LEFT Simple stencilling has made this basic angle-poise lamp more decorative without detracting from its original, clean lines.

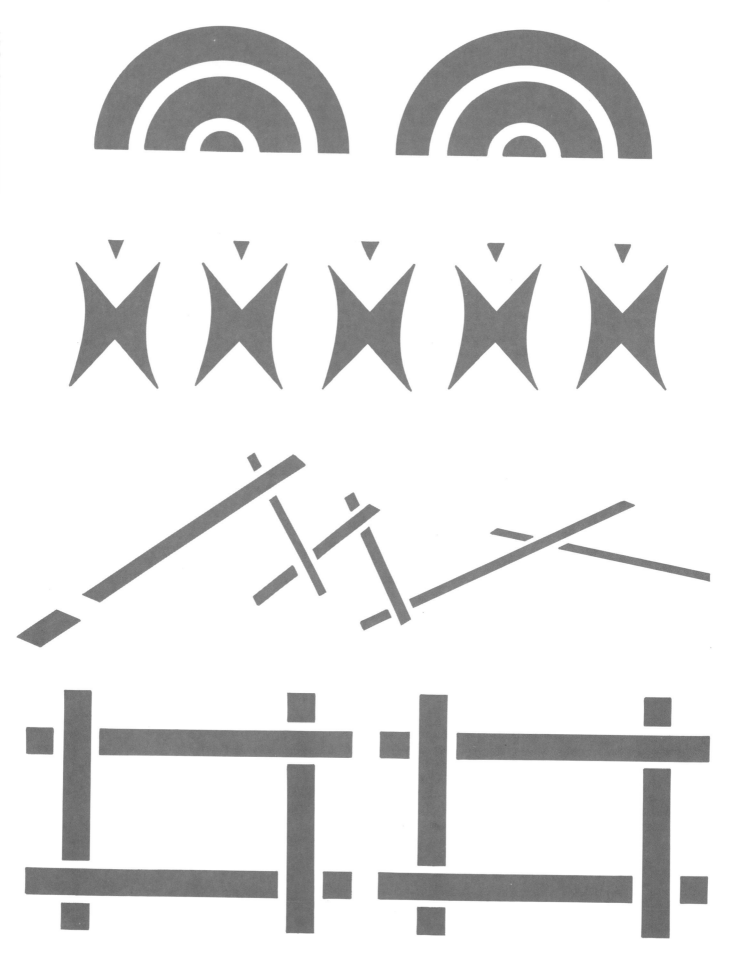

These designs will look good in modern interiors. Use the sticks border in different sizes on curtains, walls and furniture.

The brush strokes pattern can form a large motif when used in a cluster.

Naive flowers are a perfect choice to decorate a modern kitchen where a more realistic flower design would be out of place.

The sunsets motif could pattern the scalloped edge of a tablecloth or roller blind using different shades of the same colour.

Run the gateway design along the edges of cushions but use a different colour for each one.

The iced gems and other motifs are simple patterns that would look good edging a lampshade.

Decorate small pieces of furniture such as a bedside table with the corner frame design and use the speed border around a door frame in a teenage bedroom.

A border at dado rail height using the weights design would look punchy in shades of blue and green.

Add more rows or use only a single row from the crosses' pattern in a bathroom or kitchen.

The semicircle motif is extremely versatile. Use it all or just a single row. Use it upside down or on its side around a door frame. Clever use of shading techniques will make it three dimensional.

Rialto is a simple Art Deco design. Use pastel or rich colours and change the size of the motif as you use it in different areas.

The lozenge border is really three designs in one. Mix and match them around the room using soft colours in a bedroom or green and metallic gold in

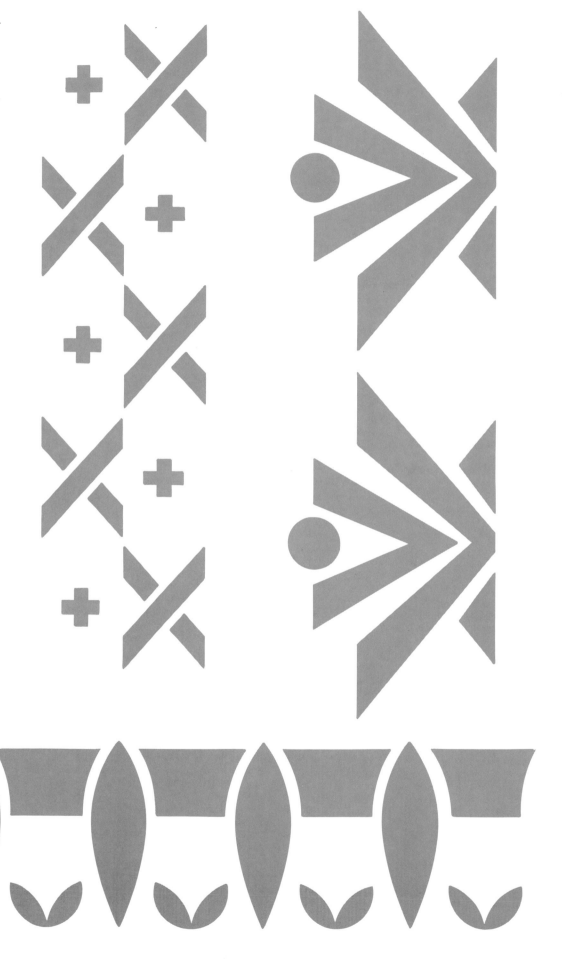

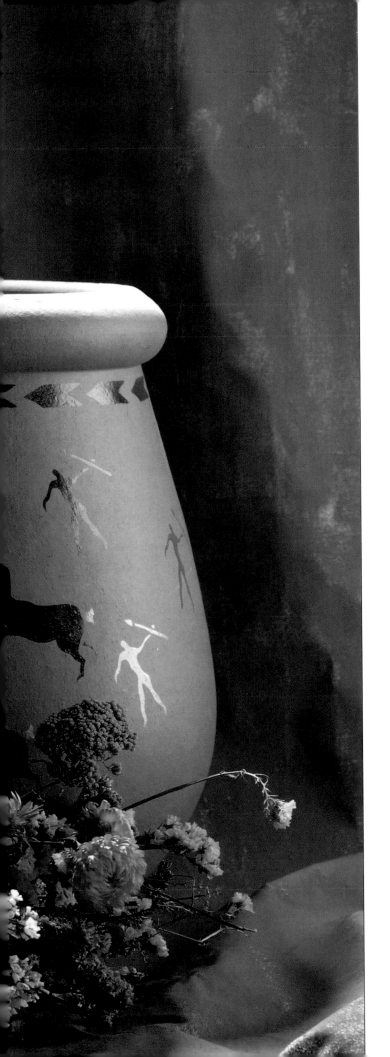

Chapter 7

AROUND THE WORLD

Brightly patterned saris and Indian temples; Navajo rugs and jewellery; Inca architecture and brightly feathered birds; Persian carpets and Caribbean fabrics. You will find that the world is your oyster when you begin to seek out designs for your stencilling projects.

PREVIOUS PAGE Giant clay pots make the perfect foil for African designs stencilled with ceramic paints.

To find a source for ethnic patterns all you have to do is take a trip around the world! Luckily, it's quite possible these days to make the journey while sitting in your favourite armchair! Seek out travel brochures and travel books in your local library about the particular countries and cultures that you admire. There are many superb books, lavishly illustrated in full colour, about almost every country in the world. Find books about national costume and jewellery as well as the history of pattern and design.

If you get the opportunity, visit as many museums as you can. You can browse around to your heart's content making little sketches of any patterns that take your interest. You don't have to produce a work of art, just something to remind you of the pattern when you get home. Some museums sell postcards of their exhibits. These can be invaluable.

Of course, if you get the chance to visit the country of your dreams so much the better. A walk around the Alhambra Gardens would provide enough source material to last for years.

Now, what do you do with your designs once you have found them? With unlimited time and money you could turn the inside of your suburban home into an Egyptian palace or a Spanish hacienda but is this what you really want?

On the other hand you may not want a solitary decoration in your chosen style, looking as much out of place in its surroundings as the single souvenir brought back from an exotic holiday.

However you could choose one room to decorate in your chosen style. If you are an aficionado of Moorish architecture you can make many elaborate borders using the tile designs typical of that culture. Make some silk cushions, stencil them in jewel bright colours and scatter them around the room. Your curtains and lampshades could be stencilled to match.

If Egyptian design is more to your taste, stencil Egyptian figures in a border or on panels on your walls. They are fairly stylised already and easily lend themselves to stencilling. The shape of the pyramid could be used to make a super three dimensional design. Try using orange or sand colours with red ochre and the green of palm leaves in your colour scheme.

Perhaps you prefer a taste of India? Again, jewel like colours abound in clothing, art and furniture. Look at paisley patterns and fabrics and the colours in a peacock feather for inspiration.

A simple mirror is given distinction with the addition of a border design based on a Persian tile. See how the design has been adapted to fit the space available on each side and corner.

Simple tile designs with their Aztec influence make a colourful feature of this otherwise dark kitchen range.

A simple African design has been used here to divide the walls in this modern bathroom. You can use ethnic designs in any setting providing you chose your colours with care.

A modern but classic lampshade has been decorated using reverse stencilling. To do this you cut your stencil pattern as usual but keep the cut out piece. This then becomes a stencil allowing you to paint around the outer edges. The same technique can be tried using found objects such as fallen leaves.

The Red Indian nations of America produce the most beautiful rugs and jewellery using natural materials and dyes. The browns of the earth, silver and turquoise could all be used in your colour palette.

Africa is a wonderful stopping off place on your armchair journey. Stylised animals and birds, jungle prints and desert colours can all be used in borders and fabric decoration. This is indeed a land of contrasts.

Russia is not the drab country we sometimes imagine! The architecture and national costumes are incredibly beautiful and well worth investigating.

Scandinavia is an area rich in tradition and pattern as are the countries of South America.

Australia is a young country in western eyes but a wealth of tribal art has been endowed to the world from the Aboriginal tribes. Their patterns are often complex with deep meanings

Five different designs have come together to create this wall hanging. Its roots are not of any one particular country but it makes a pleasing backdrop to a small tabletop collection.

and would suit a more simplistic interior style.

The intricate, interwoven designs from the Celtic countries have often been used as a basis for decoration. There are hundreds of motifs, stylised animals, birds and flowers all waiting to spark your imagination.

You can make wall hangings, in natural materials, using any design source, or stencil hangings directly onto the wall using them as a backdrop for a group of collected artefacts. This will create a small oasis to blend into your existing decorative scheme.

Stencil large pieces of fabric and use

them as throws for your sofa and chairs. You can also create wonderful rug and carpet designs on wooden floors. Look to Persian carpets and Spanish rugs for inspiration and don't forget generous tassels and fringes around the edges!

Of course pots and vases make perfect supports for ethnic designs and, since unfired ceramic paints are not permanent, you can change your style whenever you please.

Remember, when stencilling fabric use only natural materials such as silk, cotton and linen. Happily these are the selfsame materials that will add authenticity to your decoration.

Animals and birds are all part of ethnic designs from Russia to North America and South Africa. I think it would be interesting to use the eagle design as the basis for a rug or wall hanging, while the dancing bears are a perfect centrepiece for a small table with the claws border running around the perimeter.

The hunter and animals are designed in a very naive style. Imagine them coloured with deep earth shades on a throwover for your sofa and chairs. The giraffe could join all the other animals to create wonderful designs in a playroom or nursery.

You cannot fail to get a three-dimensional effect when you use the zig-zag shadow lines design.

All of the designs in this section will appeal to purer tastes. There are no frills and flowers here, although the colours can be as bright or as subtle as you choose. Use each design in its entirety or take elements from each to suit your needs. Most would create exotic border patterns for walls or floors but I think you could make some dramatic wrapping papers with these designs too. The small abstract designs would look great used on lamps and shelf fronts. Creamy curtains decorated with the zigzag pattern in shades of turquoise and yellow would cheer up a sitting room or use it to create vertical stripes on your wall to imitate geometric wallpaper. Borders don't have to be horizontal.

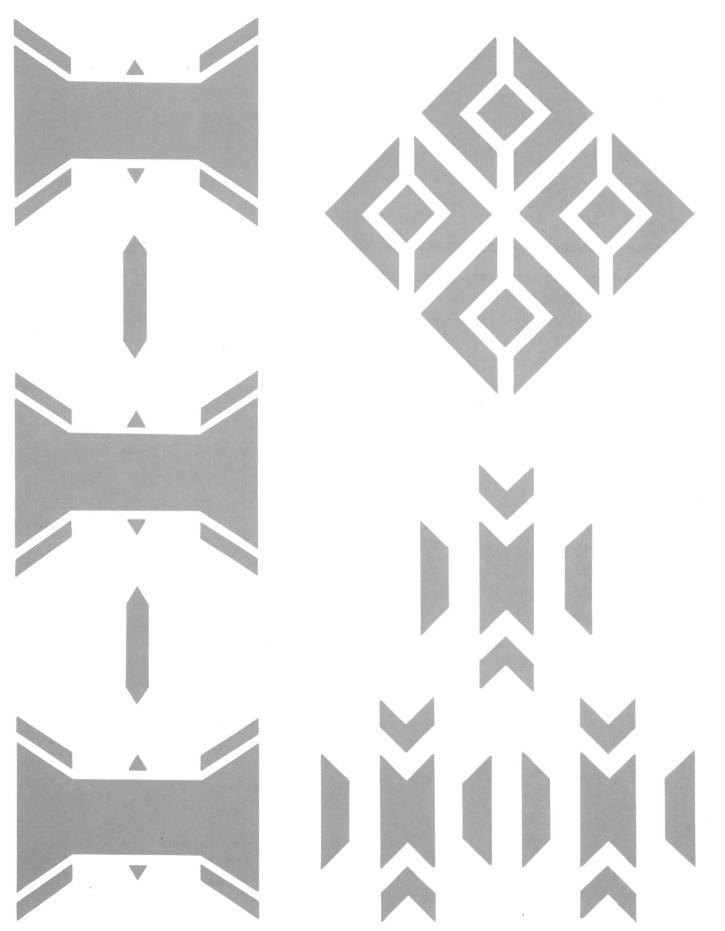

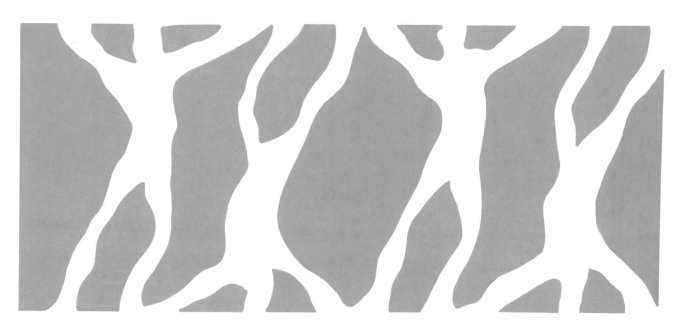

This bold African design shows a unique use of negative space. The dark cut-out shapes are interesting in themselves but when you look at the bridges in the pattern you can see naive human figures. If you want to make a border with this design you must loose the straight edges and match the pattern properly.

The chequered border would look wonderful in a sleek kitchen or hallway, while the eastern pattern would add drama to an exotic bedroom. The more simplistic pattern of squares and triangles would enhance a plain picture frame. Use the pyramid, star and diamond motifs to create interesting patterns and borders in a teenager's room. These simple styles could be used as borders or as random decoration. And they lend themselves to bold colourways which could look very dramatic.

Chapter 8

KITCHEN GARDEN

Herbs and fresh vegetables; gleaming tiles and steaming teapots; apple pies and cinnamon sticks; blackberry jam and gingham tablecloths. These are some of the sights and smells that cannot fail to evoke happy memories of mealtimes shared with family and friends.

If you've never thought of stencilling glass, here's a simple idea for beginners to try on glass storage jars. Use a motif or letters to identify the contents of the jars or play around with simple decorations.

FAR RIGHT *Cupboards beneath a window seat give both extra storage space and room for decoration. These were painted with two shades of blue then sanded to give an illusion of age. The stencil decoration, although looking rather complicated, uses just the one leaf and one bunch of grapes from the trace off patterns.*

No matter how inviting you make the rest of your home, everyone always seem to gravitate towards the kitchen. So you might as well enjoy their company and treat your kitchen, not just as a work room, but as another place for entertaining.

I often think that people are divided into two categories, those who want a highly polished, streamlined kitchen with everything in its place and those who crave stone sinks and wooden shelves with all their possessions on display.

Whichever your preference there's a place for stencilling in your kitchen.

Think of your favourite fruit or vegetable. Let's say it's an apple. Now let's find some ways for you to incorporate it into your decor. First of all, make a simple design of a single apple, then add some leaves and you've the basis for a simple border design. Elaborate a little with the addition of two more apples drawn from different viewpoints and put one behind the other to add depth. Draw in apple blossom and perhaps some small branches. Try

bending the design to make a swag and then fashion your design into a wreath. You now have all the ingredients for a decorative scheme based on one simple idea. There are borders for your walls and motifs for your kitchen units, doors and tiles. And all these designs could be put to use on your curtains as well as your tablecloths and napkins.

Try using this as a one-colour design. Paint the fruit, leaves, branch and blossom all in blue and you have a scheme to enhance both a streamlined or a country kitchen. A multicoloured scheme would soften the hard lines of stainless steel and plastic, while at the same time blending beautifully with wood.

If you have display shelves showing off your favourite ornaments you could add trompe l'oeil plates to the collection. This may sound difficult but actually it is quite easy. If you keep pots of fresh herbs in your kitchen you can add a few stencilled pots of your own. Or work on a border design based on the herbal knot garden as a background to your collection.

RIGHT *A pair of net
curtains decorated with
small bunches of cherries
will brighten up any dismal
day. It's best to use acrylic
paint to stencil onto man-
made fibres.*

BELOW *This flowering
shrub in its attractive pot
could be stencilled on a
doorway or even on the
walls of a stairway.*

Stencil corn dollies around the doorway or a border of gingerbread men for
your children to count. Cheer up your
walls at ceiling level, with stencilled
bunches of dried herbs and flowers tied
with stencilled twine or ribbon. Then
stencil trompe l'oeil nails to hang them
from for added authenticity.

If you are whimsical by nature what
about stencilling a row of apple pies
with steam rising from their funnels?
Or a fanciful border of grapes and wine
glasses.

Plain walls can be enlivened with a
mixture of motifs of several different
fruits, say cherries, pears and plums,
dotted around at random.

It may help to sit down and write a
list of all the fruits and vegetables you
can think of. You will be surprised at
how many there are. Have fun and play
around with their different shapes to
make mixed vegetable borders or a
summer fruit salad.

Next time you go shopping to your
local market or supermarket take a look
at the fruit and vegetables on display.
You can buy the subjects that take your
fancy and have the added pleasure of
eating them when you have finished
making your designs.

A good seed catalogue will provide
you with wonderful references for your
designs and a comprehensive gardening book will give valuable infor-
mation not only on how to grow the
fruit and vegetables but also give you
instructions on how to cook them. So
in these you would find both your apple
and your apple pie!

A cornucopia or horn of plenty is one design where fruit, vegetables, flowers and insects can come together quite happily. It is a very traditional theme that's especially popular at harvest time. I made one for my own kitchen, shown at the beginning of this chapter and I'm delighted with its shape and colour. Try designing one yourself using your favourite fruit and vegetables then add multicoloured butterflies and bees. You can make it as simple or as complex as you wish. It would make a marvellous motif for the walls in a room where the family gathers to eat or position it above a fireplace. Of course, you will be able to take various elements to make smaller motifs and borders to co-ordinate your room.

Here's a colourful selection of stencilled ceramic tiles to use in a kitchen or bathroom. Don't forget that they must be varnished after decoration to give them added protection.

Rows of green peas strung along the kitchen walls will be very cheerful. Don't just arrange them in straight lines but make them billow and sway.

The pepper is a simple design that could be made stronger by colouring it naturally in reds, greens and yellows.

A swag of apples, blossom and leaves would be pretty anywhere in the home but especially at ceiling height in your kitchen.

I have made the vase and leafy squares especially for use on tiles although you could use a few of the elements to make a flowery border.

A steaming teapot and dancing cups are a whimsical decoration for a tea tray or tea caddy.

The corn border could brighten up your kitchen curtains or run around a door frame. You don't have to use natural colours, try black corn onto a grey background.

Rows of bright tomatoes will make a jaunty border around your kitchen and on your storage jars.

Cherries are always a favourite motif to use anywhere in your kitchen or dining room. They don't have to be red. Try blue fruit with yellow leaves.

The pineapple is a handsome fruit and would be wonderful stencilled onto your cupboards or as a hospitality symbol over the door.

Make a simple border with the three pears along the top of your tiles. If they are plain tiles you could also decorate a sprinkling of them with the motif.

The wild strawberry would be pretty on little drawer fronts.

The grape motif is quite a large design. By careful masking, you can make several different bunches of fruit. Reverse the design every now and then you can produce a whole vine.

Chapter 9

VICTORIAN

Tartan fabrics and whitewashed walls; skirts on piano stools and antimacassars; ribbons and beads and curlicues and bows; gothic architecture and the Arts and Crafts movement. The Victorian era lasted a long time, and spanned a huge variety of tastes and styles.

PREVIOUS PAGE Large fans and ribbons decorate this panelled screen and there's a smaller version of the same design used as a border. It's the perfect accessory for a Victorian style bedroom which you could make or pick up at a second-hand shop.

The Victorian age in England, was relatively peaceful and brought great changes to the country due to a rapid succession of new inventions and scientific discoveries. The Pre-Raphaelite movement produced beautifully detailed, realistic paintings. On the other hand, the age saw the emergence of the Arts and Crafts Movement with its emphasis on more simple forms of decoration. Much of the furniture of the period was heavy and sombre but surprisingly it was decorated with the most exquisite patterns.

The era saw the beginnings of mass production, so decorative goods were more affordable to everyone. This, coupled with the fact that the Victorian era was comparatively recent, means that there is a vast amount of original material to draw on for your designs. Many catalogues of furniture, wallpaper and clothing are still in existence as well as contemporary magazines with their intriguing advertisements. There are also many books devoted to period lifestyles from which you can get ideas.

This ornate Victorian oil lamp needed a minimum of embellishment to enhance its looks. A small design stencilled around the globe in ceramic paints is the perfect finishing touch.

The Art Nouveau movement began towards the end of Queen Victoria's reign in the 1890s and because of its graceful, flowing lines it is a favourite with many people. This period is also extremely well catalogued and you will find that each source country, be it England, France or Germany, brought its own nuances to the movement.

If you have no original period features in your home try stencilling your own. A frieze at dado rail level will effectively split your wall in two. You could then stencil an all-over pattern either above or below the frieze while leaving the rest perfectly plain. You could also take the frieze over the door and down to skirting board level.

Here a group of mismatched pictures has been united with stencilled bows, cord and tassels. The tassels appear to be swaying slightly to give a little life to an otherwise static scene.

Stencil a mock picture rail around the room. Then fix your pictures securely to the walls but stencil chains from them so that they appear to be hanging from the rail.

You will find that stencilling is the ideal medium with which to visually alter the proportions of your rooms. The addition of dado rails and picture rails divides the walls and therefore reduces their height while adding interest. You can change the look of your furniture too. Wardrobe and cupboard doors can all be given the flavour of any era, be it Victorian or Edwardian, with the addition of stencilled moulding from that period. Walls, doors and panelling could also be given the same treatment.

Stencil flower designs onto lace-edged antimacassars and carry the theme onto arm guards for your sofas and chairs. You can then turn your attention to the fireplace. If it is not authentic you can start the renovation by stencilling your own tiled surround.

Plain wooden floorboards are the perfect surface for a border carpet design using only three motifs. The same design would look equally good up a staircase, along a hallway or on a landing.

The nineteenth century was not the age of fitted carpets so think about stencilling a carpet onto your wooden floor. This will be infinitely less expensive than the real thing. You can either make a complete carpet or an edging carpet with a real rug in the centre giving you the best of both worlds.

Stencil a small set of picture frames on the wall and fill them with silhouettes, stencilled by you of course, or with floral designs. If stencilled in a vertical line they could be 'held in place' by a stencilled ribbon.

Imitate glass engraving on your bathroom windows by stencilling them with a design using car spray paints. Use the same design on the wall around mirrors, sink and bath. You could even carry the design onto towels. The best way to do this is to stencil cotton fabric and sew it as a decorative band around the edge of the towel. Still in the bathroom your glass lampshade could look more distinctive with a matching motif.

A decorated screen will give instant style to your Victorian bedroom. Screens are quite easy to make with strong plywood. You could also try making a screen with wooden battens and the stencilled fabric of your choice. Be careful to avoid ending up with something looking like a hospital screen!

The top of your dressing table could be covered with lacey runners and mats stencilled directly onto the surface for a trompe l'oeil effect that never needs laundering.

Most of us would not wish to be transported back to the Victorian era but, there are many ways to bring echoes of its splendour into your home.

Lace trimmed dressing table mats are deocrated with Art Nouveau style poppies. The small mats are patterned with a single, co-ordinating design.

The tulip border would make a super edging for a tablecloth or curtains.

Bunches of violets would look very pretty scattered on bed linen or dressing table mats and could even form a frieze around a bed head.

Add imitation carvings to your furniture with the curly motif. Good shading will make them look three dimensional.

The alpine clematis is a very graceful flower which I think would look delightful used to personalise stationery. The sinuous curving lines of the poppies would look very attractive as a frieze or try stencilling them onto the glass of your bathroom windows using car spray paint.

The small heart motif, painted in a single colour is just the thing to stencil onto drawer fronts to enhance fancy handles, while the elaborately curled bellflower motif would look very smart as a random wall decoration in a traditional dining room. Paint the design in a slightly darker shade of your wall colour.

The fuchsia motif would look delightful as a corner decoration on a mirror. Paint either on the wall or on the mirror itself or use to create a simple pattern for a jewellery box.

Use the striped bow as a pretend support for your favourite pictures. You can extend the 'tail' if you want this to hang behind a vertical row of pictures. Cut two overlays, one for the ribbon area and one for the stripes.

Stencil the oval picture frame, singly or in groups, on your wall and fill them with stencilled flower posies such as the violets in this section. You can also use the oval shape on its own, on wardrobe doors, again pattern with a simple motif. Brighten up a plain lampshade with the tiny abstract motif along its edges or put the design in just the corners of a small table.

With suitable variations in size the bow, cord and tassel have many uses. Run the cord up the stair wall as an imitation bannister rope, or curl the designs around the wall at picture rail height.

The arum lily is reminiscent of Art Nouveau designs of the Victorian era and would make a wonderful tile pattern.

Pretty parasols are a good subject for a border design in a feminine bedroom.

Chapter 10

FLOWERS AND PLANTS

Trailing ivy and wisteria; butterflies and bees; pot plants and trellis work; sweet peas and canes; colourful birds and blue skies. The world outside is a wonderful arena of bird and animal life and of plants both cultivated and wild. It is up to you to decide what elements you want to bring into your home.

PREVIOUS PAGE *Would you believe that an old wooden trunk could look so attractive, simply by patterning it with a trailing flower and leaf stencil? Take special care to choose the right section of your stencil when turning corners.*

A magnificent stencilled image of a vase crammed with flowers has been framed and hung on a wall. To tie it into the decorative scheme of the room a frieze was created using elements from the picture and stencilled along the wall at dado rail height.

This delightful clematis has been worked using only the simple leaf and flower patterns from the Design section of this chapter. The pot has been given a decorative band to break up what would have otherwise been too large an expanse of terracotta.

Imagine being cooped up in the house on a cold, wet, miserable wintry day. All your pot plants are out of season and there is not a flower in sight. Out of the window you can't even see your winter garden for the drizzle.

What can you do about it? Why not pick up your brushes and paints and start stencilling?

The place to start could well be the room in which you spend most of your time. This may be the sitting room, a home office or a games room. Hallways and landings tend to be the most ignored areas and could well be the site for your indoor garden, brightening your day as you move from room to room.

Now you have choices to make. Do you make a grand splash and stencil a large climbing plant wending its way up the walls or make a collection of smaller plants to brighten up a corner of the room? You could of course take up both options!

If you have a conservatory you have the perfect site for your artistry. Stencil flowering plants or ivies on the wall. You will find that they intermingle wonderfully with any real plants. They will also have the added advantage of requiring no attention, unless of course you wish to add to their growth! And for that exotic touch you could stencil tropical birds or butterflies hovering around the plants.

Perhaps you live in a basement or have rooms in your home that receive little light, even in summer. Here again, stencilling can come to the rescue.

Stencil a row of clay pots along a shelf and 'fill' them with spring flowering bulbs such as hyacinths and daffodils. The flowers can then be changed to suit the season or your mood.

If you place a small table against the wall you can stencil a vase onto the wall so that, at first glance, it fools the eye and appears to be standing on the table. Then you can fill the vase with a bunch of stencilled wild flowers or a more formal arrangement of blooms. This would look wonderful in a bedroom with matching vases on two bedside tables. To make your bedroom really pretty you could even make up a small motif from elements of the bunch of flowers and stencil it at random on your walls and soft furnishings.

A large stencil at ceiling height can look very dramatic. Here ribbons and bows are entwined with trailing flowers.

A plain white dressing table and wardrobe were too austere to complement this sunny, south-facing bedroom. After suitable preparation they were both rag-rolled with pale pink paint to soften their appearance. A dog rose and sweet ivy stencil was then applied which in turn softened the lines of the furniture.

A screen can be useful in almost any room and is the perfect piece of furniture on which to try out your talents. It also gives you two surfaces to decorate so you can ring the changes simply by turning it around. It would make a super room divider with different themes on each side to suit both halves of the room.

Of course, you don't have to take up stencilling on a grand scale to bring the outside in. Take a bedroom for example. You can stencil floral motifs onto dressing tables, wardrobes and chests. Light airy curtains stencilled with butterflies or shutters patterned with wild flowers will all add to the mood.

If you have an ivy or other plants climbing up the outside of your house why not bring it inside too? Start by stencilling a few tendrils on the window surround and carry them onto the walls and curtains. Design a circlet and stencil it onto the wall over your bed. There is no end to the possibilities.

Your bathroom could become home to a collection of plants from the rainforest, which would look even more realistic as the steam rises from your bath.

A stencilled collection of exotic orchids, lit by a simple spotlight, would make a marvellous focal point in any sitting room.

If you have an indoor swimming pool these designs are ideal. You can take any of the ideas here and make them work for you. The walls will provide you with a large canvas on which to exercise your skills and imagination.

To find ideas for stencil designs you need go no further then the garden. You may have several favourite plants that you could live with all year round. If so, make a small collection of photographs and drawings to give you a reference point. Look at books on garden ornament to find the correct pots to hold your artistic endeavours. You could use your own vases from which to make designs and group the real with the false! Books on both indoor and outdoor gardening will be invaluable as will specialist books about tropical plants.

If you want your stencilled plants to be as realistic as possible look at your source material carefully. Some plants climb by twisting to the left and some to the right. This and other similar details are easily overlooked and will only annoy you when you discover the error.

A small whitewood tea tray has been brought to life with two garden favourites, the exotic fuchsia and the cheerful bluetit.

A group of garden pots stand drying in the sun before being taken indoors to decorate a garden room.

Stencil this elaborate fuchsia on a coffee table or above your doorways using either pastel or vibrant colours to suit your decor.

The cheeky bluetit could perch on any branch or twig in your stencil designs.

Busy bees and butterflies in sparkling colours will brighten up your walls or give extra realism to stencilled flowers.

The dog rose, violet, and ivy design is very adaptable. You can use all the elements separately to produce an extremely feminine room.

Design a classical
border with the urn motif
and add ivy leaves to the
design.

Both the pots can be
used to hold stencilled
bunches of flowers or large
indoor plants but remember
to adjust the size
accordingly.

The bay tree would look
right at home beside a
kitchen doorway.

Make a group of pot
plants by stencilling them
along the wall above a shelf
or use them to decorate
door panels.

The clematis flowers, leaves
and buds can be used as
freestanding motifs or
made up into borders as
you wish. With a little
planning you can create a
whole plant as shown in the
photograph in this chapter.

The trellis design will
work well on its own in any
room in the house but you
can add a climbing plant
either real or stencilled.

Chapter 11

FESTIVE

Holly and mistletoe; Christmas crackers and party hats; balloons and greeting cards; Easter eggs and birthday gifts; wedding days and anniversaries. There are so many festive occasions in our lives. In these days of commercialisation it is extremely satisfying to produce a gift, card or decoration that is of your own design.

What could be more simple than this trio of Christmas tree decorations made in thick card sprayed with gold paint? The same stencil has been repeated on each card using a different colourway each time.

Not many of us want to stencil our home with holly and ivy entwined with red Christmas ribbon, or with baubles sparkling with silver glitter. However, there are still lots of ways to decorate your home for the Christmas season without going to these extremes.

An eye-catching wreath of holly, mistletoe and hellebore would look wonderful stencilled onto a piece of wood and cut out in the same way as the flower circlet described in the Rustic Charm chapter. You could use it year after year, to decorate your front door or make matching wreaths, one for each side of the chimney breast and link with ribbons or natural ivy.

Decorations for the Christmas tree could be made with different designs stencilled onto card using metallic paints, adding glitter as a final touch. This is a job that all the family would enjoy. If you stencil small fabric sacks or stockings they could be hung from the tree holding tiny gifts or chocolates. Do remember not to put real lighted candles on the tree.

The traditional Christmas dinner is still a favourite event, gathering together families and old friends and it's a time to show off your seasonal stencilling to advantage. You can decorate a tablecloth, napkins and napkin rings especially for Christmas.

It's a good idea to stencil a large circular or rectangular motif in the centre of the table. Then turn your attention to the place settings. If you have two sets of napkins you could stencil a smaller version of the central design around the edges of one set and use as napkins proper. While the second set could be used as place mats with the same motif stencilled in a circle to surround the dinner plate.

It's an idea that you could repeat for all festive occasions. Different designs could be incorporated for birthdays, special anniversaries or wedding celebrations. You could also consider stencilling seating cards and even decorative menus.

Welcome your guests at Christmas with a cheerful table setting and they will never want to leave. This is a good example of simple stencilling having impact while blending into its surroundings.

If there is a wedding in your family you could make a marvellous set of wedding stationery for the bride and groom. Use their favourite flower as the focal point for the design. I recently created a stencil for my future sister-in-law who had never stencilled a thing in her life before. She used it to pattern her wedding stationery and had the added satisfaction of doing all the work herself. The floral motif could be extended into the wedding album by stencilling the photo mounts, making an extra special design for the wedding portrait.

A pretty sampler is a lovely way to celebrate the birth of a new baby. But if, like me, you are quite useless with needle and thread, you can stencil the

ABOVE *Making your own greeting cards is an ideal introduction to stencilling. This pretty collection of cards would cover many festive occasions.*

RIGHT *Piles of presents have been gift wrapped in stencilled paper and plain boxes have an extra flourish with seasonal designs. You could make matching gift tags and greeting cards too.*

This charming rose design has been stencilled onto a piece of canvas where it will make a beautiful subject for embroidery. With a change of colour it has become a delightful picture waiting to be framed and hung on the wall. Both would make charming gifts for a birthday or anniversary.

sampler instead. Try using some of the designs from the Baby Talk chapter, either onto fabric or watercolour paper then mount in a frame. Obviously this idea could be extended to include special birthdays and anniversaries.

If, however, you are a whiz with a needle and embroidery threads, you could stencil a spray of roses onto a piece of silk, then enhance the three-dimensional effect by adding some embroidery to the flowers. Even more depth can be added by allowing the design, whether stencilled or stitched, to spill over onto the picture mount.

The ability to change the colour of the roses to suit the occasion, red for a

ruby anniversary or yellow for a wedding, is very useful.

There is no need to scour the specialist shops in vain for that extra special card when you can design your own to suit every occasion. Wrapping paper and gift tags can also be made to match. This is another area where you can encourage your children in their artistic endeavours by designing a special set of stencils for them to use when sending birthday cards to their friends.

The best source material you can turn to here is a knowledge of your friends. Hobbies and pastimes such as fishing or wine-tasting can be the starting points for many designs.

The pretty spray of daffodils is an ideal subject for an Easter greeting card or small embroidered picture.

Stencil Easter eggs onto pieces of card and hide them around the house for a simple hunt the egg game, with prizes for the winners of course!

The flowered hat is specially for Easter but it would also make a pretty border in a little girl's bedroom. This beautiful rose motif would make a lovely decoration for a plain tablecloth at every place setting, while the bubbly champagne and glasses would help you to announce any happy occasion. Silver bells are the ideal design to adorn wedding invitations.

I have made lots of Christmas stencil designs for you to choose from. Look at them carefully as some will need a second registered stencil for the decorative details. They are all ideal for matching greeting cards, wrapping paper and gift tags or special decorations for your tree. Larger versions of the stockings, candles and baubles could also be used to decorate your living or dining rooms. This is an activity for all the family to share.

A B C D E F G

H I J K L M N

O P Q R S T U

V W X Y Z

I have designed two
styles of lettering and
numbers. The bolder
version is ideal for spelling
out a child's name or for
the recognition games
described in Baby Talk.
Use the more flowing
version to put messages on
your cards and tags. Both
styles would look attractive
if used to make a special
sampler to commemorate a
birth or marriage.

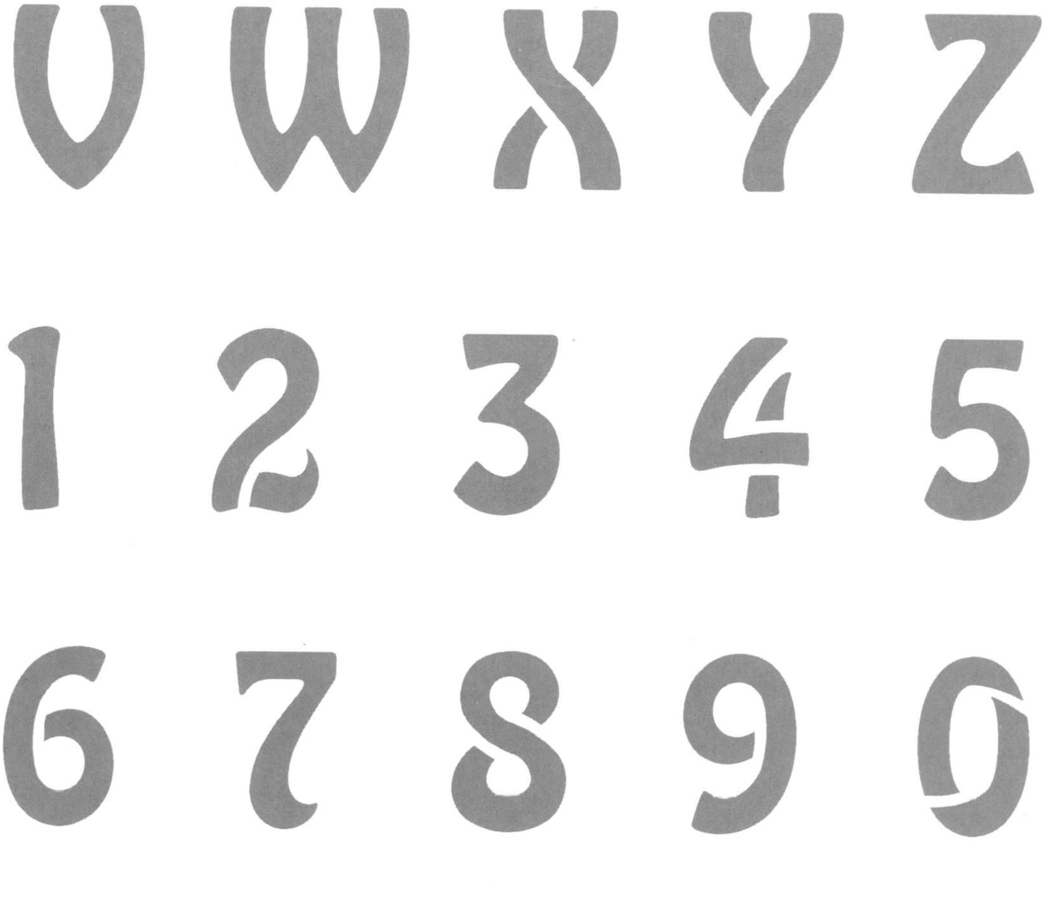

1 2 3 4 5

6 7 8 9 0

A B C D E F G

H I J K L M N

O P Q R S T U

V W X Y Z

1 2 3 4 5

6 7 8 9 0

MATERIALS
AND TECHNIQUES

WHAT IS A STENCIL?

A stencil is any paper cut out with holes or 'windows' through which you can paint colour on to a chosen surface. The stencil can be as simple or intricate as you wish. From a design on a single sheet, or overlay, used with just one colour, to several overlays using many colours.

Each part of the stencil has a role to play. The holes form the pattern and the spaces between, called bridges, or ties, separate the different elements and give a sense of realism and depth to the design.

MATERIALS

CARD: The most traditional material for making a stencil is manila card. This is a heavy gauge card that has been soaked in linseed oil to make it waterproof. Ideally it should be used with oil based or spray paints, because water based paints will eventually make it soggy and unusable.

The advantage of using manila card is that it is easy to cut. Its main disadvantage is that you can't see through it, which is important when you line up your design for a repeating border, or a design comprising of more than one overlay. The answer is to cut registration marks into the stencil or notches into the edges of the stencil, which can be matched with each overlay. Alternatively you can simply select one or two elements of the design and cut them out of each overlay. But remember to only paint them once.

ACETATE: Draughtsmen's acetate is the best type for stencilling. But always choose the right weight for the job. If it is too stiff it will be difficult to cut and won't bend around corners easily, if it is too thin it will tear. Acetate is shiny on one side and slightly opaque on the other. It is long lasting, easy to clean and you can see through it for easy registration. Draw directly onto the opaque side of the acetate with a pencil and paint onto the shiny side, but remember that the image will be reversed when you turn the acetate over. Wipe your stencil clean from time to time to prevent a build up of paint in the windows.

PAPER: Providing you are not going to put your stencil to extensive use, you can make it from heavy paper or cardboard. Both are easy to draw on, easy to cut and have the added bonus of being inexpensive. However, unless you use heavy tracing paper, you will not be able to see through your stencil for registration purposes.

METAL: Stencils made from thin brass are long lasting and easy to clean, but you can't see though them for registration and they are difficult to cut.

OTHERS: You can use a piece of lace or paper doilies to create a pretty stencil and interesting, if delicate effects on walls and furniture. A few coats of varnish will strengthen them long enough for limited use.

Several designs have come together in this hallway to decorate the walls and emphasise the rich colour of the mahogany doors.

EQUIPMENT

BRUSHES: It is easy to recognise the traditional stencil brush by its round stock and flat-cut bristles. It's a specialised design which hasn't changed for centuries. You can buy brushes in a variety of sizes, each one designed for a particular task. The largest brushes, with the biggest stock, are suitable for floors and those stencils with larger windows in their design. The smallest brushes are for the tiniest details. I prefer to use the largest brushes possible, as they seem to blend the colours so much better.

As stencilling continues to increase in popularity, brushes and other tools of the trade are readily available from art supply shops and specialist stencil stores. If you have difficulty in finding stencil brushes you can use an ordinary paint brush, but unfortunately they are not so adept when you're blending colours. It is also possible to use an old shaving brush, but you must cut the bristles flat across the top. Do not use an expensive brush as the bristles will be too soft.

Be sure to clean your brushes throughly when you have finished work. If you look after them they will last a lifetime.

SPONGES: Try experimenting with a sea sponge to apply the colour. This will give a beautifully dappled effect to your stencilling. And a mixture of brushed and sponged stencilling on one project will add texture to your chosen design.

PAINTS: If stencillers of bygone days could see the selection of paints and the range of colours available today they would be positively green with envy!

You should have no trouble at all in finding the right paint in the right colour for whatever project you have in mind. You can use many types of paint for stencilling, depending on the effect you wish to achieve. All you have to do is match the paint to the surface, whether plaster, wood, fabric or glass, and use common sense. For example you should always use non-toxic paints in children's rooms.

ACRYLICS: These are available from all good art supply shops and come in a wonderful array of colours, including pearl and metallic finishes. They are fast drying and can blend easily. As acrylic paints are water based you can thin them with water, and you can clean your brushes quite easily afterwards with warm soapy water. The fast drying qualities of acrylics make them ideal for stencilling.

As stencilling requires very little basic equipment, it is worth investing in a good cutting utensil and brushes. The surface to be decorated will dictate the paints to be used.

STENCIL PAINTS: These are also water based, but are normally sold in pots and are more liquid in form than most artist's acrylics. As they are specially made for stencilling they are very fast drying so you can get on with your project much quicker. Brushes may be cleaned in warm water.

OIL PAINTSTICKS: As the name suggests this is oil paint, but it is specially formulated into sticks that look like chunky wax crayons. They are very easy to use and the colours blend beautifully. As the crayons are 'self healing' they do not dry out and will last for simply ages. The only drawback is that as the paint is oil based, you will have to clean your brushes with white spirit before washing them in soapy water.

CREAMS: Stencil paints in cream form are a new addition to the range of paints available to the stenciller. They are a solid paint in a jar so you can hold them in your hand while stencilling and just dip in your brush when it needs reloading. Cream paints are suitable for use on all surfaces including fabric.

SPRAY PAINTS: Many professional decorators use car or other spray paints for stencilling. They are available in a large range of colours including metallic. No brushes are required as you just spray the paint directly on to your chosen surface. More often than not you can use just one overlay, as the wonderful effects are obtained by subtle use of the spray. The great disadvantage of spray paints is that they can be very messy, so you must protect surrounding areas with newspaper to stop the paint spreading. They are also quite difficult to use until you get the pressure on the nozzle just right. Do not be discouraged by all this as the final results can be quite stunning.

FABRIC PAINTS: There are many different makes of fabric paint available which can be used in the same way as acrylics and other water based paints. Many can be fixed by ironing or by tumble drying. You can of course stencil on to most fabrics but the natural fabrics such as cotton, linen and silk are the best.

CERAMIC PAINTS: These paints are for use on tiles, pottery vases, tableware and other ceramic items. Unless you have access to a kiln only use those paints that don't need firing. Bare in mind that these paints are for purely decorative purposes and, as such, will not stand up to a lot of washing or the dishwasher. So don't think about decorating the dinner service just yet!

JAPAN PAINTS: These are oil based paints which are also extremely fast drying making them perfect for stencilling. The range of colours however is not extensive.

OTHERS: You can use any kind of paint for stencilling as long as you match the paint to the surface. Beautiful effects can be achieved with watercolour paint however, this should be thickened by mixing with a little acrylic paint. I often use it un-thickened on heavy watercolour paper and let the colour bleed. Not very traditional, but different!

All water based household paints can be used but they often take too long to dry, which can be a disadvange if you are trying to decorate your room with a mutlicoloured border or frieze.

Wood stains and varnishes also give interesting effects. You can obviously use them on wood but clear varnish mixed with a little oil paint can be quite beautiful as a decoration on glassware.

Always follow the manufacturers' instructions. Some paints, as well as solvents, can be dangerous!

As you become more
confident you will be able to
stencil large images, floors
and ceramics with ease.
Although the designs in
this room are all quite
different, their colours are
reflected in the patchwork
tablecloth.

PREPARATION OF SURFACES

As with all forms of decorating the surface must be prepared to accept the paint you have chosen. If you don't do the groundwork you will not get good results. Dust and grit under the stencil will prevent it from lying flat and make the paint bleed under the stencil paper.

WALLS: Remove all traces of old wallpaper and fill in any holes. It's not necessary for walls to be perfectly smooth, it all depends on the look you want to achieve. Allow newly decorated walls to dry out thoroughly before stencilling. You can stencil onto bare plaster but treat it first with clear universal sealant.

PAINTED SURFACES: You can paint on to virtually any painted surface providing it is properly prepared. Gloss paint must be 'keyed' by sanding first. You should not have to seal your stencil with varnish unless it is to receive heavy use. Varnish the whole surface, not just the stencilled area as varnish tends to yellow slightly with age.

WOOD: Remove any wax or varnish and strip off old paint using a proprietary stripper following manufacturers' instructions. If the surface is very rough sand it first with a coarse sandpaper, followed by a 'wet and dry' sandpaper to give it a final smooth finish. Don't forget to always paint with the grain.

GLASS: The only prerequisite here is that the glass should be clean, dry and free of grease.

FABRIC: Fabric should always be prewashed to remove any trace of size and then ironed. The size can cause the paint to bleed and ruin your stencilling.

WOODEN FLOORS: Using coarse sandpaper then grading down to a 'wet and dry' sandpaper, sand the floor, with the grain, to give a 'key'. When you've finished, vacuum and wipe down with a lint-free cloth. For an old floor, you may have to use an industrial sander, to get a smooth surface and to get rid of any old varnish and polish. Sand the corners and edges by hand. When you have finished stencilling, seal the floor with at least two coats of colourless varnish and your work of art, will last for years.

METAL: Remove old paint using the correct proprietary stripper. Remove any rust with a wire brush and sand the metal with steel wool. Stencil directly onto the metal or paint first with a metal primer. Oil based paints are best to use on metal as they help prevent rust and remember to seal your stencilling, with a coat of clear varnish.

CERAMICS: Ensure the surface is clean, dry and free from grease, then stencil directly onto the surface using ceramic paints again seal with a proprietary varnish to give your work a longer life.

PLASTIC: Before stencilling always 'key' the surface with fine sandpaper. You can also paint the plastic first, then stencil onto the paint.

PAPER: You can stencil on to most types of paper, although a textured wallpaper is not an ideal surface as it will break up your design.

LINING UP

The following instructions for lining up your stencils are guide lines only. You can position a border with great scientific precision, only to find that it looks rather odd in a room that is not perfectly square.

CENTRE-POINTS: All you need are two pieces of string. Pin the end of one piece of string in one corner and pin the other end in the opposite corner. Repeat the procedure with the second piece of string in the two remaining corners. The place where the strings cross is your centre point.

VERTICALS AND HORIZONTALS: To find the true vertical of a wall you will need a plumb line. Coat the string with chalk and attach the plumb line, fairly high up, on the wall. Let the plumb line settle. Then, holding the plumb weight steadily against the wall with one hand, 'twang' the string. This will leave a line of chalk on the wall.

A spirit-level and a ruler or a tape measure are all you need to find a horizontal line. Decide at what height from the floor you want your stencil. Measure this height at intervals along the wall with chalk or a soft pencil. Then attach a piece of string to the wall at both sides so it runs along the marks and draw in the horizontal line.

BORDERS AND FRIEZES: Always begin in the middle and work outwards. You may find that the design will fit the space available using the exact number of repeats. If the design almost fits the space, you can stretch it or compress it slightly as you work, but if there is just too much space left over, you can take some of the elements from the stencil and make a corner motif.

ROUNDING CORNERS: You may find it easier to treat each wall individually and use a corner motif on each one. This method works rather nicely around a door frame, putting the corner motif at the base of the frame and again at the top corners.

An acetate stencil will bend into a corner and you will be able to carry on stencilling without interruption. Don't forget that if you are stencilling a border around a whole room your design will have to join together at some point, so be prepared!

MITRING CORNERS: Draw a pencil line at 45 degrees into the corner. Then put a strip of masking tape against your pencil line and stencil up to the tape. Move the masking tape to the other side of the pencilled line and match the stencilling into the corner. As this can be tricky, always do a dummy run on a piece of paper before attempting the real thing.

MOTIFS: You can place motifs on the wall or floor in a random manner using your eye as a guide. You can, if you wish be more precise and draw up a grid. To do this simply attach one end of a piece of string to the centre of one wall, at floor level, and the other end to the centre of the opposite wall. Mark the position of the string on the floor, move the string an equal distance along the two walls and make the next set of marks. Continue until you have all the lines you need and then repeat using the two remaining walls. Now you can place the motifs as desired.

STENCILLING TECHNIQUES

To fix your stencil to the wall you can use low tack masking tape positioned along the outside edges of the stencil. This will keep it secure but won't remove your paint surface. Alternatively you can spray the back of the stencil with spray adhesive. This also holds the stencil in place but allows you to peel it away from the surface and reposition more easily. Always use in a well ventilated room.

APPLYING THE PAINT: The best advice I can give you is to practice your stencil on a piece of paper first. The other golden rules are, always use a dry, clean brush and don't overload it with colour as this will cause the paint to seep under the edges of the stencil paper and smudge the design. A dirty brush will taint your colours.

USING PAINT STICKS: These have a 'sealing skin' over the surface to prevent the paint from drying out. To obtain the colour and break the seal, simply rub the point of the stick onto a separate piece of acetate. Pick up the colour on your brush by rubbing it gently into the paint, using first a clockwise and then an anticlockwise movement. Hold your brush at right angles to the stencil and apply the paint using the same circular strokes. Always start by applying the paint around the edges of the cut out areas first. This will create a lighter area in the middle, as the colour is worked off, and is the first step in shading your design.

USING STENCIL PAINTS: Don't use the paint straight from the pot or tube because you will invariably overload your brush. Put a little of the paint on to a saucer and if necessary thin down with the appropriate thinning agent to get better consistency.

Dip the brush into the paint wetting only the ends of the bristles. Now take most of it off again on a paper towel or newspaper by rubbing the bristles gently clockwise and then anticlockwise onto the paper. When your brush is practically dry, apply the paint gently to the stencil, again using the circular movements. Begin painting at the edges of the cut-out areas working to the centre to give a shaded effect.

USING FABRIC PAINTS: Make sure that your fabric is laid out flat, with a layer of absorbent paper underneath as some lightweight fabrics will allow paint to seep through. This is the one occasion when you can use a damp brush because the fabric will absorb a lot of moisture.

The procedure now is exactly the same as for water based paints. However, I recommend using spray adhesive to hold the stencil in place as you will not be able to remove any paint that seeps under the edges.

USING CERAMIC PAINTS: When applying this paint it is better to use a stippling motion. Hold the brush at right angles to the stencil and by flexing your wrist, make a gentle dabbing motion with the brush onto the cut-out areas.

USING SPRAY PAINTS: Practise with the spray paints before you commit yourself to your project, as it takes some time to produce the gentle 'whoosh' that indicates the pressure on the nozzle is just right.

Hold a piece of cardboard, as a guard, at an angle against the part of the stencil you are trying to paint and spray towards that. The paint will just drift onto the stencil and the windows will not become clogged. You need just the lightest film of paint with each coat.

If you use a stencil with a single overlay you may get some overspill from one colour to the next, but sometimes this creates beautiful effects.

SHADING: While it is perfectly acceptable to stencil with simple colours, say green for the leaves and blue for the flowers, you will get a much more professional effect if you add shading to the design, giving it realism.

Shading can be added merely by putting colour on the outer edges of the pattern, leaving a paler area in the centre, rather like a patch of sunlight. You can also get a similar effect by painting lightly all over the design in one colour then add another, stronger coat around the edges. Several different colours may also be used for shading. For example, when shading a blue flower, I'll also add a hint of purple to the shadow area. Where a leaf curls behind a flower, the flower colour can be used to shade the leaf. After all this happens naturally! So, if you stencil a complex pattern, don't worry if some of the colour spills over into other parts of the design.

CUTTING YOUR STENCILS: Use a new blade in your knife or scalpel for each stencil and change it regularly. A blunt blade will rip your stencil rather than cut it cleanly. Put your stencil material on the cutting base and place one hand on the acetate or manila card to keep it steady. Take the craft knife or scalpel and make firm, smooth cuts, always towards yourself but away from the hand steadying the stencil. Cut each window in one stroke for the cleanest edge. Always begin at the centre of the design and work outwards, cutting the smallest windows first. If you cut the largest ones first the stencil will lose strength and subsequent cuts may tear the bridges. Leave a border of about 2ins (5cm) around the cut-out pattern to stop paint spilling over the edges.

MENDING DAMAGED STENCILS: Just put a strip of masking tape over both sides of the rip and simply recut that area.

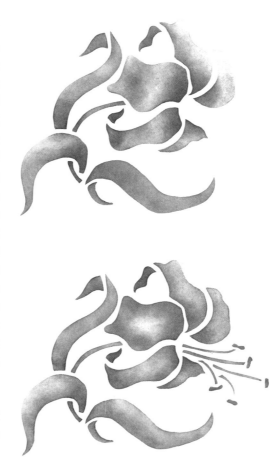

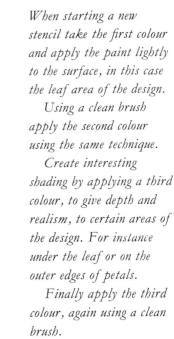

When starting a new stencil take the first colour and apply the paint lightly to the surface, in this case the leaf area of the design.

Using a clean brush apply the second colour using the same technique.

Create interesting shading by applying a third colour, to give depth and realism, to certain areas of the design. For instance under the leaf or on the outer edges of petals.

Finally apply the third colour, again using a clean brush.

STEP BY STEP INSTRUCTIONS

Trace your chosen design either from our trace off designs, or from a reference book, on to good quality tracing paper. Use a soft pencil. If you are cutting your stencil in acetate, trace the design directly on to the non-shiny side of the acetate. Remember the image will be reversed when you stencil as you always paint over the shiny side of the acetate. To avoid image reversal, place the design under glass and the acetate on top of the glass. Cut the acetate following the lines visible through the glass.

If the design is not the right size for your purposes you may need to reduce or increase its size. To do this take a sheet of tracing paper drawn with a squared grid then trace the design. Take another sheet of grid paper with either smaller or larger squares, as required, and copy the design, square by square on to the new grid.

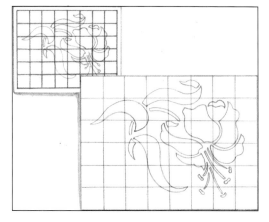

If you are making your stencil from manila card you will need to trasfer the traced design on to the card. Do this by rubbing the reverse of the tracing paper with a very soft pencil. Then place the tracing paper, right side up, on to the card and rework the outline using a hard pencil to transfer the image on to the card.

To cut a manila card or acetate stencil simply lay the acetate or card on a sheet of glass (with the edges bound in masking tape to prevent accidents) or on a self-healing cutting board. Using a new blade and scalpel or craft knife cut out the stencil using firm, smooth cuts. Always cut towards yourself but away from the hand holding the stencil. Cut each window in one stroke for the cleanest edge.

Position the stencil onto the surface you are decorating. Secure with either low tack masking tape or spray adhesive. The latter helps you reposition the stencil several times without damaging the surface, so is probably more helpful for beginners. Always use in a well ventilated room.

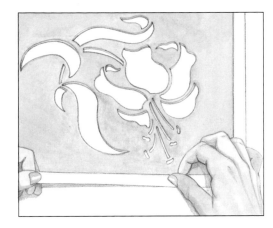

Apply a little paint to a dry brush. Work most of the paint off the brush on to a dry paper towel or newspaper. It is much better to apply the paint in several thin layers rather than in a single thick one which will only cause the paint to seep under the stencil paper and smudge your work.

Holding the brush, like a pencil, in one hand and supporting the stencil with the other apply the paint to the cut-out areas of the stencil using light circular movements, in both clockwise and anticlockwise directions. Build up the colour and shading gradually.

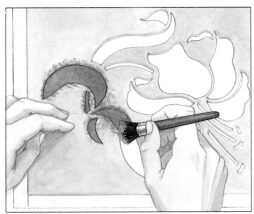

When you have completed the stencil, gently remove it from the surface. Using the registration points reposition on the surface and continuing stencilling until you have completed the required length. For simple designs you can reposition the design by eye only. Clean away any build up of paint on the stencil as necessary.

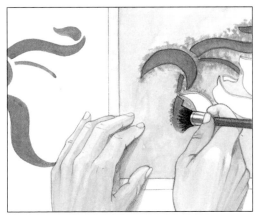

If you have more overlays for additional colours position each one in succession over the stencilled area. Again use the registration points. You should not have to wait long before using additional overlays as most stencil paints dry rapidly. Always remember to use a clean brush for each new colour.

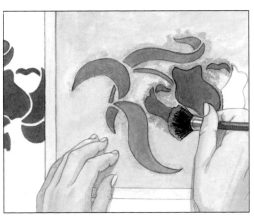

INDEX

The page numbers in *italics* refer to the illustrations.

ACKNOWLEDGEMENTS

I would like to thank Pat and Basil Fowler, Nancy and Tony Roberts, and Peter and Alice Burden for allowing me to stencil in their homes and Rhona Mote for the use of her props. A special thank you must also go to Eileen Berry who did all the needlework, helped out with props and lent her enthusiasm to the project.

Lastly, I wish to thank my husband for his photographs and his understanding.

The author and publishers are grateful to the following for permission to reproduce copyright photographs: Jon Bouchier pages 7, 12, 47, 54, 77, 111, 133, 136; Robert Harding Picture Library 24, 25, 33, 67, 69; The Stencil Library 90; Elizabeth Whiting & Associates 32, 120.

LIST OF SUPPLIERS

U.K.
Elrose Products Ltd.
20/21 Heronsgate Road,
Chorleywood,
Hertfordshire,
WD3 5BN.

The Stencil Store,
91 Lower Sloane St,
London SW1 W8DA.

Lyn Le Grice Stencil Design Ltd.
Bread Street,
Penzance,
Cornwall TR18 2EQ.

Stencil Decor,
Eurostudio Ltd,
Unit 4,
Southdown Industrial Estate,
Southdown Road,
Harpenden,
Herts AL5 1PW.

The Stencil Library,
Nesbitt Hill Head,
Stamfordham,
Northumberland,
NE18 0LG.

U.S.A.
The Stencilers Emporium,
P.O. Box 536,
Twinsburg, OH 44087.
U.S.A.

Stencil Artisans League Inc.
P.O. Box 920190,
Norcross, GA 30092.
U.S.A.

S.A.L.I. is a friendly, non-profit making organisation whose members work to promote stencilling throughout the world. Members are kept up to date with all the latest products and techniques.

AUSTRALIA
The Stencil House,
662 Glenferrie Road,
Hawthorn,
Victoria 3122.